West

The Earth's Weather

Rebecca Harman

www.heinemann.co.uk/library
Visit our website to find out more information about Heinemann Library books.

To order:
☎ Phone 44 (0) 1865 888066
🖹 Send a fax to 44 (0) 1865 314091
💻 Visit the Heinemann Bookshop at www.heinemann.co.uk/library to browse our catalogue and order online.

First published in Great Britain by Heinemann Library, Halley Court, Jordan Hill, Oxford OX2 8EJ, part of Harcourt Education. Heinemann is a registered trademark of Harcourt Education Ltd.

Editorial: Melanie Copland
Design: Victoria Bevan and AMR Design
Illustration: Art Construction and David Woodroffe
Picture Research: Mica Brancic and Helen Reilly
Production: Duncan Gilbert

Originated by Chroma Graphics (Overseas) Pte. Ltd
Printed in China by WKT Company Limited

The paper used to print this book comes from sustainable resources.

ISBN 0 431 01300 4
09 08 07 06 05
10 9 8 7 6 5 4 3 2 1

British Library Cataloguing in Publication Data
Harman, Rebecca
The Earth's Weather: changing patterns and systems (Earth's Processes)
551.6

A full catalogue record for this book is available from the British Library.

Acknowledgements
The Publishers would like to thank the following for permission to reproduce photographs: Corbis, **p.28**; Press Association/Eric Gay **p.19**; Press Association/LM Otero **p.21**; Press Association **p.23**; Press Association/Diario la Republica **p.25**; Press Association/Yesikka Vivancos **p.26**; Science Photo Library/NASA **p.10**; Science Photo Library/Alex Maclean **pp.17, 18**; Science Photo Library **p.27**; SPL **p.7**; Still Pictures/Weatherstock **p.4**; Still Pictures/Qinetiq LTD **p.5**; Still Pictures/Jim Wark **p.6**; Still Pictures/Philippe Hays **p.11**; Still Pictures/Ted Mead/WWI **p.12**; Still Pictures/Carlo Dani & Ingrid Jeske **p.16**; Science Photo Library **p.20**; Still Pictures/Weatherstock, **p.22**.

Cover photograph of lightning reproduced with permission from Corbis.

The Publishers would like to thank Nick Lapthorn for his assistance in the preparation of this book.

Disclaimer
All Internet addresses (URLs) given in this book were valid at the time of going to press. However, due to the dynamic nature of the Internet, some addresses may have changed, or sites may have changed or ceased to exist since publication. While the author and Publishers regret any inconvenience this may cause readers, no responsibility for any such changes can be accepted by either the author or the Publishers.

Contents

Words appearing in the text in bold, like this, are explained in the Glossary.

What is weather?

Have you ever been woken up during the night by thunder and lightning? You might have got up and watched the lightning strikes through the window. You may have counted the seconds in between seeing the lightning flash and hearing the thunder to see how far away the storm is. A **thunderstorm** is just one example of a **weather** event.

The weather is what is happening in the **atmosphere** around us, in one place at one point in time. The atmosphere is a blanket of air that surrounds the Earth and is held down by **gravity**. All weather takes place in the atmosphere. It may be a snowstorm in Edinburgh, a sunny sky above Sydney, or a **hurricane** off the coast of Cuba.

Being caught outside in a thunderstorm can be a very frightening experience.

Is weather the same as climate?

You should be careful not to confuse weather with **climate**. The climate of an area is the total of all the day-to-day weather there over about 30 years. So climate is the general weather an area will experience. For example, if an area has a lot of rain, such as the west coast of Scotland, then we say it has a wet climate, even though it may not rain every day. This is different from describing the weather of the area, which can change every day, and sometimes many times in one day!

A satellite image is a photograph taken from space. In this image you can see that the atmosphere forms a blanket of air around the Earth.

All the information you need on the weather is outside. Go outside and have a look at the sky. You may see the Sun, you may see clouds, you may see rain, hail, or snow. You may feel cold air and wind blowing in your face. This is all weather, and next time you look, it may be different.

Did you know?

The weather is always changing, in some areas very quickly and sometimes violently. A hailstorm can last just five minutes.

All weather takes place in the atmosphere.

What are the ingredients of weather?

There are three main ingredients in weather. These are **air pressure**, **temperature**, and **humidity**. Just as you mix ingredients together to make a cake, these weather ingredients get mixed together in the atmosphere to form different types of weather.

Did you know?

Scientists who study the weather are called **meteorologists**. In much the same way as a doctor looks at the condition of a patient to work out what is wrong with them, so meteorologists look at the condition of the atmosphere to work out what will happen next. Most weather presenters on television are meteorologists. They do not just tell us about the weather, they study it as well, and try to **predict** what it will do.

Meteorologists preparing to launch a weather balloon into a tornado in Kansas, USA.

What is air pressure?

As the atmosphere rests on the Earth's surface it pushes down on it. This is air pressure. Cold air is heavier than warm air, so we say cold air has a higher pressure. Air pressure is measured using an instrument called a **barometer**. Differences in pressure from one area to another produce winds. Winds blow from high to low pressure.

A thermometer measures how hot or cold the air is. In the Celsius scale, water freezes at 0 °C and boils at 100 °C. In the Fahrenheit scale, water freezes at 32 °F and boils at 212 °F.

What is temperature?

The temperature of a place is how hot or cold it is. This is measured using an instrument called a **thermometer**. A thermometer records the temperature in degrees Celsius (°C) and degrees Fahrenheit (°F). Differences in temperature cause differences in pressure. If air becomes warmer it will rise, resulting in lower pressure. If air becomes colder it will sink, resulting in higher pressure.

What is humidity?

Humidity is the amount of moisture in the air. The moisture is an invisible gas called **water vapour**. If humidity is high, there is a good chance of **precipitation** (rain, sleet, snow, or hail). The humidity depends on the temperature of the air, as colder air can hold less moisture than warmer air.

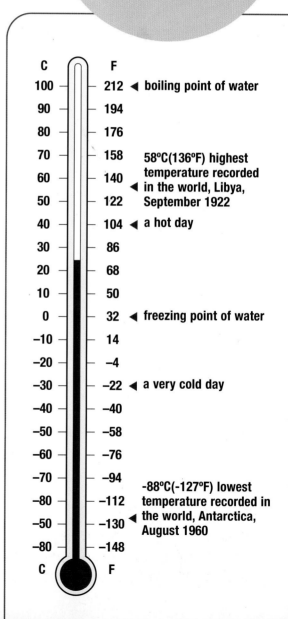

C	F	
100	212	◄ boiling point of water
90	194	
80	176	
70	158	58°C(136°F) highest
60	140	temperature recorded
50	122	◄ in the world, Libya, September 1922
40	104	◄ a hot day
30	86	
20	68	
10	50	
0	32	◄ freezing point of water
−10	14	
−20	−4	
−30	−22	◄ a very cold day
−40	−40	
−50	−58	
−60	−76	
−70	−94	
−80	−112	-88°C(-127°F) lowest
−50	−130	◄ temperature recorded in the world, Antarctica, August 1960
−80	−148	
C	F	

What creates the Earth's weather?

During the day, the Sun shines on the Earth, warming the surface and the atmosphere above it. However, the Sun does not shine evenly on the Earth's surface.

At the **Equator** it is warm all year round. The Sun is almost directly overhead, so heating is concentrated in a small area. This is why it is so hot in countries close to the Equator.

Further north or south of the Equator the Sun is not directly overhead. It is at an angle in the sky, so the heat is spread over a larger area. This means the ground and atmosphere receive less heat, so it is cooler than at the Equator.

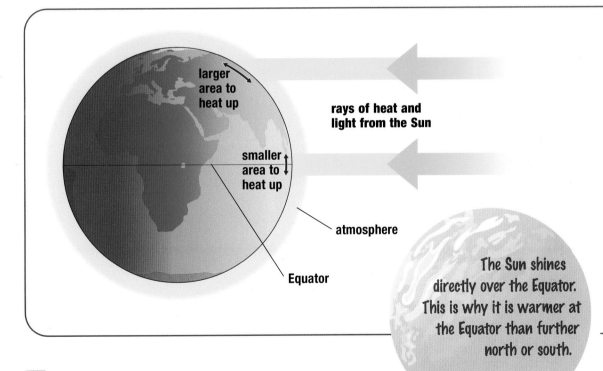

larger area to heat up

rays of heat and light from the Sun

smaller area to heat up

atmosphere

Equator

The Sun shines directly over the Equator. This is why it is warmer at the Equator than further north or south.

Did you know?

The Sun is 150 million kilometres (93 million miles) from Earth. It provides the **energy** to create the Earth's weather. This energy is in the form of light and heat.

The weather is the result of this uneven heating of the Earth's surface. Heat always moves from where it is hot to where it is cold. Warm air from the Equator moves towards colder parts of the world and heats them up. The warm air is blown by winds to the colder areas north and south of the Equator.

Winds do not just move air across the Earth, they also move air up and down in the atmosphere. When the air close to the ground at the Equator is heated, it becomes lighter than the air above it, so it rises. As the warm air rises, colder, heavier air sinks to take its place.

As a result of all this, air at the Equator is heated, rises up and moves to the north or south. The space left is filled by cold air that is blown towards the Equator. This cold air is then heated and the cycle begins again. This cycle of moving air creates all the weather we see on Earth.

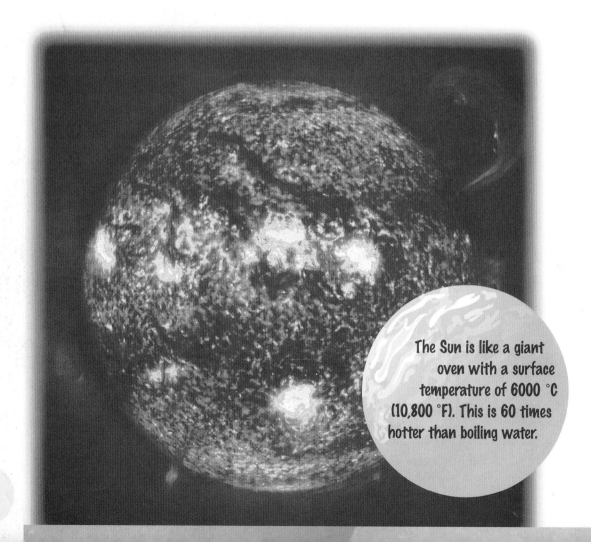

The Sun is like a giant oven with a surface temperature of 6000 °C (10,800 °F). This is 60 times hotter than boiling water.

Why does the weather change?

Changes in the weather are caused by changes in the pressure, temperature, and humidity of the air. This happens as the air moves from warm to cold areas and from cold areas to warm ones.

This movement of air produces two main pressure systems:

- areas of low pressure, called **lows**
- areas of high pressure, called **highs**

Each has very different types of weather.

Low pressure systems are also called **depressions**. These are areas of the atmosphere where pressure is lower than in the surrounding areas because air is rising. As the air rises it cools. Cold air cannot carry as much moisture as warm air, so some of the water vapour in the air **condenses**. This means it changes into tiny drops of water. This produces clouds and rain.

London often has bad weather as a result of low pressure systems.

Did you know?

Low pressure systems can be huge. Just one low may cover the entire western half of Europe.

11

High pressure systems are also called **anticyclones**. These are areas of the atmosphere where pressure is higher than in the surrounding areas because air is falling. This has the opposite effect to a low. As the air falls, it is warmed. This produces sunny, dry weather.

Highs and lows are continually forming, moving across the Earth and dying away. Lows usually last for only a few days. In the United Kingdom the weather can change very quickly because of lows blowing in from across the Atlantic Ocean. This means that one summer day may be dry, warm, and calm, while the next day may be wet, cool, and windy. Highs sometimes last a lot longer. When this happens they are called blocking anticyclones, because they force all other weather to travel around them. The Sahara Desert is one example of a place that has high pressure and sunny skies for most of the year.

A high pressure system brings clear skies. The Sun will heat the ground up quickly during the day, but at night it will be cold as there are no clouds to stop the heat escaping.

What is an air mass?

An air mass is a very large area of air with similar pressure, temperature, and humidity. Air masses are so big that they can cover half of the United States.

An air mass forms when air stays still for a long time (a few weeks to a few months) over one area. This area is called the source region. The air mass takes on the same pressure, temperature, and humidity as its source region. For example, air over the Arctic Ocean will become cold and wet, while air over the Sahara Desert will become warm and dry.

Air masses drift slowly away from their source regions for thousands of kilometres. As an air mass moves, it keeps the same pressure, temperature, and humidity, because it does not mix with other air masses. This means it will change the weather in the areas over which it moves. For example, if an air mass formed over northern Canada moves south over the United States it will bring cold, dry weather with it.

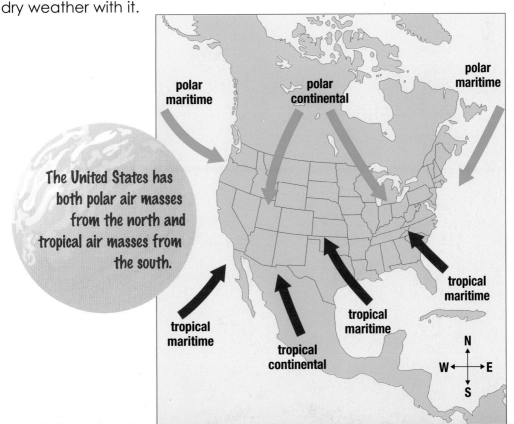

The United States has both polar air masses from the north and tropical air masses from the south.

polar maritime

polar continental

polar maritime

tropical maritime

tropical continental

tropical maritime

tropical maritime

N
W E
S

Did you know?

There are four main types of air mass, depending on their source region:

- Polar continental – this type of air mass forms over land in **polar regions**. These are very cold ice and snow covered regions, such as northern Canada and Alaska. It produces very cold, dry weather in winter and cool, pleasant weather in summer.

- Polar maritime – this type of air mass forms over oceans in polar regions, such as the Arctic Ocean. It produces cool, wet weather in the areas it travels over.

- Tropical continental – this type of air mass forms over land in **tropical regions**. These are very hot areas, such as northern Mexico and the Sahara Desert. It produces hot, dry weather with clear skies.

- Tropical maritime – this type of air mass forms over oceans near the **Equator**, such as the eastern Pacific Ocean and the Caribbean Sea. It produces warm, wet weather.

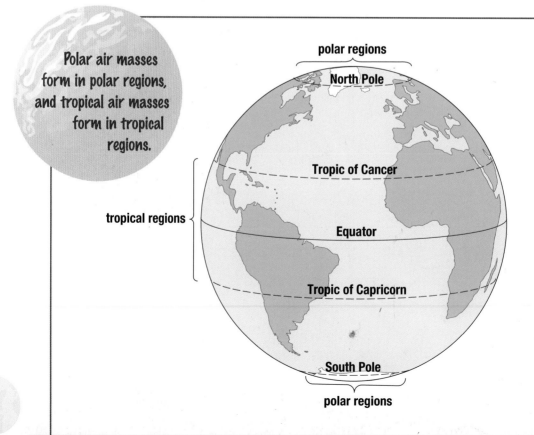

Polar air masses form in polar regions, and tropical air masses form in tropical regions.

polar regions

North Pole

Tropic of Cancer

tropical regions

Equator

Tropic of Capricorn

South Pole

polar regions

What is a weather front?

Air masses do not mix with other air masses. This means that a boundary forms between air masses when they meet. This boundary is called a **front**. At the front, one air mass tries to move the other out of the way so that it can continue its journey.

As polar air masses move towards the Equator and tropical air masses move towards the poles, they usually meet over North America, the North Atlantic, and Europe. When they bump into each other this results in an exciting display of weather activity. This is why the weather is so changeable in these areas.

When a tropical air mass with its warmer, lighter air moves towards a polar air mass with its colder, heavier air, the warm air rises up over the cold air. This is because the warm air is lighter than cold air. As the warm air rises, it cools and condenses to produce clouds and rain. The place where this happens is called a **warm front**.

At the warm front, warm air rises up above cold air producing a wide band of clouds and rain. At the cold front, cold air cuts under the warm air, forcing it to rise. This produces a narrow band of clouds and rain.

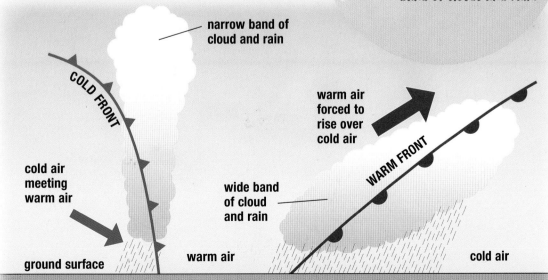

narrow band of cloud and rain

COLD FRONT

warm air forced to rise over cold air

WARM FRONT

cold air meeting warm air

wide band of cloud and rain

ground surface

warm air

cold air

When a polar air mass with its colder, heavier air moves towards a tropical air mass with its warmer, lighter air, the cold polar air moves under the warm tropical air, forcing the warmer air to rise. As the warm air is forced up, it cools and condenses to form clouds and rain. The place where this happens is called a **cold front**.

Air masses and fronts are invisible, but they produce an endless display of weather that sweeps across the sky.

Did you know?

Because of the clouds produced along fronts, meteorologists can work out where the fronts are. They can mark them on weather maps and satellite images.

Polar continental air masses can bring cold, dry weather to areas like this in Quebec, Canada.

What is hazardous weather?

Sometimes pressure, temperature, and humidity can produce very violent weather events. Unexpected weather events can have serious effects on people's lives. The thunderstorm you thought about at the beginning of this book is one example of a **hazardous** weather event. Other examples include violent **tornadoes** and hurricanes.

What are thunderstorms?

Thunderstorms are huge clouds accompanied by lightning, thunder, strong winds, and heavy rain. They form when warm, wet air rises and condenses to form huge, towering clouds. Thunderstorms may take from a few minutes to one hour to form.

A small cloud can develop into a huge thunderstorm in a matter of minutes.

Lightning is caused by a build-up of static electricity in a thunderstorm cloud. It is like the static electricity you produce when you rub a balloon on your jumper and then stick it to a wall. The electricity causes a giant spark (lightning), which heats the air to an incredible 30,000 °C (54,000 °F). This is five times hotter than the surface of the Sun! The rapid heating causes the air to expand explosively and this is heard as a loud bang (thunder).

If lightning strikes close by, the thunder will be heard at the same time. If it strikes further away you will hear the thunder a few seconds later, because light travels faster than sound. Lightning usually strikes the highest point, so it is dangerous to be on a hill or standing under a tree during a thunderstorm.

Lightning tends to strike the highest point in an area. Here it is striking the Eiffel Tower in Paris, France.

The heavy rain produced by thunderstorms may lead to **flash floods**. These happen when very heavy rain falls over a small area in a short period of time. Flash floods are very dangerous. They cause damage to homes and crops and kill over 100 people in the United States each year.

This flood in Texas, in the United States, was caused by extremely heavy rain during a thunderstorm in 2004.

What are tornadoes?

Tornadoes are often produced by thunderstorms and they sometimes look like huge elephant trunks hanging down from thunder clouds. They are the most violent weather events on Earth.

A tornado is a funnel shape of spinning air. It can be 100 to 600 metres (328 to 1968 feet) across, with low pressure at the centre. Wind speeds are often over 200 kilometres per hour (124 mph) and can reach 500 kilometres (310 mph) per hour. This is faster than the world's fastest trains.

Tornadoes are quite small – most are smaller than a football pitch – and do not last very long. Most only last for a few minutes, but cause an enormous amount of damage. They travel along a tornado path for about 7 kilometres (4 miles) and only cause damage in this path. A tornado may destroy all the houses on one side of a street, leaving the other side completely untouched.

Being faced with a tornado, like this one in South Dakota in the United States, can be a terrifying experience.

When the funnel touches the ground, the strong winds suck up everything in its path, including trees, animals, cars, and even people. It can carry them hundreds of metres before dropping them to the ground. A tornado that hit North Carolina, USA, in November 1992 carried a school bus over 70 metres (230 feet) without killing any of the pupils on board.

Tornadoes occur in many parts of the world, but are very common in the United States. Here, there are over 700 tornadoes each year. They occur mainly in the "Tornado Alley", which stretches from Texas to Nebraska. They form in this region because the warm, moist air needed to form thunderstorms is found here. In May 1999 a tornado ripped through Oklahoma City, destroying thousands of homes and killing 48 people.

Did you know?

If a tornado forms above water, it is called a water spout. If a tornado forms above a desert, the funnel sucks up dust and is called a dust devil.

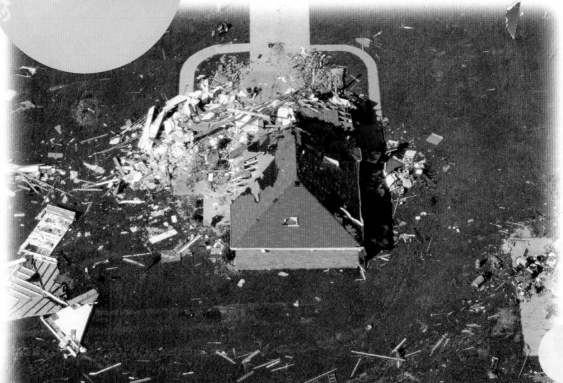

Tornadoes can cause huge damage, as seen in this area of Kentucky, USA.

Hurricanes

Hurricanes are similar to tornadoes, but they are much bigger and they form over the sea. They often travel thousands of kilometres before they hit land.

Hurricanes are large low pressure systems of spiralling air, with huge clouds, strong winds, and heavy rain. They are usually around 650 kilometres (404 miles) wide. The wind speeds are often more than 160 kilometres (99 miles) per hour and can reach 300 kilometres (186 miles) per hour sometimes. The wind produces huge waves, up to 10 metres (33 feet) high, which can completely swallow a ship.

Hurricanes form over warm seas close to the Equator. They are easy to recognize on satellite images because the clouds are grouped in a spiral. The centre of the spiral – called the eye – is cloud-free. However, it is not easy to predict where a hurricane will go. A hurricane heading directly for land may suddenly turn away and continue its journey across the ocean.

From above hurricanes look like giant whirlpools of clouds.

Hurricanes last for many days, but when they hit land they quickly die down as they lose energy. But before this they can cause a large amount of damage. This is because of high winds and huge waves called **storm surges**, as well as heavy rain, which produces flooding.

Hurricanes often occur in the Caribbean, Central America, and south-east United States. In September 2004 Hurricane Ivan struck the small island of Grenada, killing 34 people and damaging most of the houses on the island. A prison was also destroyed, and many of the prisoners escaped. The hurricane then continued through the Caribbean. Its 200-kilometres-per-hour (124 miles-per-hour) winds caused huge problems in many of the islands and killed 70 people. Ivan then hit the south-east coast of the United States, causing heavy rainfall and flooding. Many roads, bridges, and buildings were damaged and 52 people were killed.

Did you know?

A hurricane is called a typhoon along the east coast of China and a willy willy along the north coast of Australia.

This is just some of the destruction caused by Hurricane Ivan in 2004.

What is El Niño?

El Niño is an event that affects the weather in many parts of the world.

Winds blowing across the Earth create **ocean currents**. Usually in the Pacific Ocean there is a cold current in the east and a warm current in the west. The cold current is called the Peru Current, and it flows north along the west coast of South America. The cold current contains many **nutrients**, and so provides food for lots of fish.

In December every year, a warm current replaces the cold Peru Current for a few weeks. This is called El Niño. The warm water contains few nutrients, so fishing is poor at this time of year.

During an El Niño event, unusually warm water along the coast of Peru causes devastating weather events in other parts of the world.

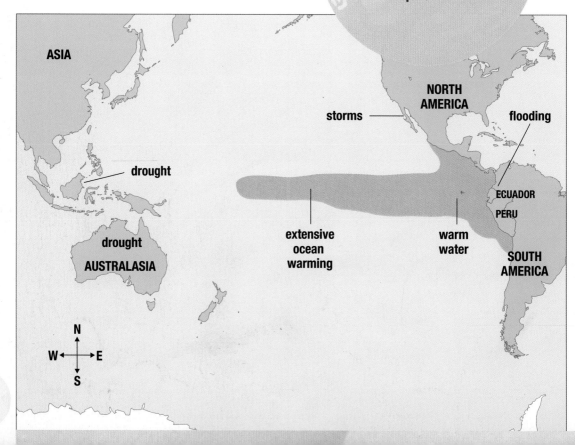

ASIA

NORTH AMERICA

storms

flooding

drought

ECUADOR

PERU

extensive ocean warming

drought

AUSTRALASIA

warm water

SOUTH AMERICA

N
W ← → E
S

Every three to seven years, El Niño conditions last for months rather than weeks. When this happens, the normal situation in the Pacific Ocean is reversed. The water in the east becomes warm and the water in the west becomes cold. The warmer water off the coast of Peru causes extreme weather conditions in different parts of the world. Nobody knows why this happens. A very severe (long lasting) El Niño in 1997–1998 caused the worst flooding Peru had ever seen. It also caused **drought** in Indonesia, southern Africa, and Australia. A drought happens when there is not enough rain. It is very serious because without rain, many crops are ruined, and so less food is made for people and animals to eat.

Did you know?

El Niño means "boy child" in Spanish. The event is called this because Jesus was born at Christmas, the same time of year as El Niño happens.

The 1997–1998 El Niño event caused extreme flooding in Peru.

25

How do weather forecasts help us?

We have all seen the weather forecast on television. We use it to help us decide what to wear and what to do that day. To make weather forecasts, meteorologists at over 10,000 **weather stations** throughout the world need to constantly check the weather. The difficult nature of weather means that it is not easy to predict what will happen, so weather forecasters can sometimes get it wrong!

Weather forecasts can also be used to give warnings about hazardous weather conditions. These warnings allow people to be prepared, and many lives and homes may be saved. With the help of ship reports, aircraft reports, and satellite images, the movements and strength of hurricanes, thunderstorms, and tornadoes can be carefully watched.

Meteorologists use computers to help them predict the weather.

If it looks like one of these hazardous weather systems will strike an area, a severe weather warning is issued. A hurricane warning is given when a hurricane is within 24 hours of reaching an area. This gives people time to evacuate (leave the area). A tornado warning is given when a tornado is spotted. This usually gives people only a few minutes to take shelter, but it may be enough to save their lives.

Unfortunately, weather forecasting is very difficult! The forecasts and warnings can be wrong, which may result in people being evacuated for no reason from an area. As our understanding of these weather events increases, improved forecasts should become available to more people.

This area of North Carolina in the United States has been evacuated following a warning about Hurricane Ivan in September 2004.

Conclusion

The weather is what is happening in the atmosphere around us, in one place at one point in time. It is always changing, in some areas very quickly, in other areas very slowly. Changes in the weather are caused by changes in the air pressure, temperature, and humidity of the air as it moves from place to place.

If air remains over one place for a long time, an air mass will form. Where one air mass meets another, a front will form. Both air masses and fronts are invisible, but they produce an endless display of weather.

Sometimes the conditions of pressure, temperature, and humidity in the atmosphere result in very violent weather events, such as thunderstorms, tornadoes, and hurricanes. These unexpected extreme events can cause much destruction and loss of life.

The difficult nature of weather means that weather forecasters find it hard to predict what will happen, so they can sometimes get it wrong. It is important to improve our understanding of the weather, because if severe weather warnings can be issued in time, many lives may be saved.

The atmosphere is about 640 kilometres thick and completely encircles the Earth.

Fact file

Scale	Wind speed	Description	Effects
0	60–120 km/hr (37–75 mph)	Weak	Tree branches broken, signs damaged
1	121–180 km/hr (76–112 mph)	Weak	Trees snapped in half, windows broken
2	181–250 km/hr (113–156 mph)	Strong	Large trees uprooted, mobile homes destroyed
3	251–330 km/hr (157–206 mph)	Strong	Trees blown down, cars overturned, walls removed from buildings
4	331–420 km/hr (207–263 mph)	Violent	Buildings destroyed
5	421–500 km/hr (264–313 mph)	Violent	Cars and buildings moved over 100 metres (328 feet), large metal structures damaged

Scale	Wind speed	Description	Effects
1	120–150 km/hr (75–94 mph)	Weak	Damage to trees
2	151–170 km/hr (95–106 mph)	Moderate	Some trees blown down. Some damage to roofs of buildings
3	171–200 km/hr (107–125 mph)	Strong	Large trees blown down. Mobile homes destroyed. Some damage to buildings. Flooding at the coast. Evacuation of coastal areas
4	201–250 km/hr (126–156 mph)	Very strong	Large amount of damage to buildings. Flooding up to 10 kilometres (6 miles) from the coast. Evacuation of coastal areas
5	Over 250 km/hr (Over 156 mph)	Devastating	All trees blown down. Buildings blown down. Evacuation of many areas

Glossary

air mass large body of air with similar pressure, temperature, and humidity

air pressure force of the atmosphere pushing down on the Earth

anticyclone area of high pressure, also called a high

atmosphere blanket of air that surrounds the Earth

barometer instrument used to measure air pressure

climate type of weather an area usually experiences

cold front front where cold polar air cuts underneath warm tropical air, forcing it to rise

condense water vapour (a gas) changing into tiny drops of liquid water

depression area of low pressure, also called a low

drought weather conditins caused when there is very little rain

El Niño warm ocean current that replaces the cold Peru current on the west coast of South America in December

energy power that is used to provide heat

Equator imaginary line drawn around the middle of the Earth

flash flood flooding that happens very quickly due to heavy rain during a thunderstorm

forecast predict what will happen in the future

front boundary between two different air masses

gravity force that keeps things on Earth

hazardous dangerous

high area of high pressure, also called an anticyclone

humidity amount of moisture in the air

hurricane very intense low pressure system of spiralling air, with huge clouds, strong winds, and heavy rain

low area of low pressure, also called a depression

meteorologist someone who studies the weather

nutrient food that plants and animals need

ocean current flow of water in an ocean caused by winds blowing the surface of the water

polar region very cold region close to the North or South Pole

precipitation rain, sleet, snow, or hail

predict say what will happen in the future

satellite image photograph taken from space

storm surge huge wave caused by a hurricane

temperature measurement of how hot or cold a place is

thermometer instrument used to measure temperature

thunderstorm storm with towering clouds, lightning, thunder, strong, gusty winds, and heavy rain

tornado funnel-shaped mass of spinning air with low pressure at the centre

tropical region very hot area close to the Equator

warm front front where warm tropical air rides up over cold polar air

water vapour water in the air in the form of an invisible gas

weather condition of the atmosphere in one place at one point in time

weather stations laboratories where meteorologists record the weather

Index

More books to read

A Pirate Adventure, Andrew Solway (Raintree, 2005)
Awesome Forces of Nature: Howling Hurricanes, Louise and Richard Spilsbury (Heinemann Library, 2004)
Earthwise: Weather, Jim Pipe (Franklin Watts, 2004)

Titles in *The Earth's Processes* series include:

Hardback   0 431 01298 9

Hardback   0 431 01299 7

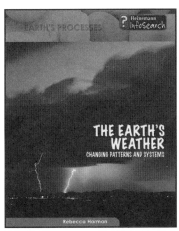

Hardback   0 431 01300 4

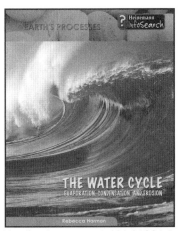

Hardback   0 431 01301 2

Hardback   0 431 01302 0

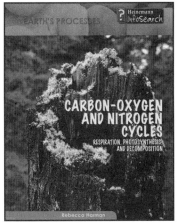

Hardback   0 431 01303 9

Find out about other titles from Heinemann Library on our website www.heinemann.co.uk/library